SAVVY FRIENDS

PRESS

TURKEY
SAVVY

How to
stuff a bird, feed fortunate guests,
and make lifelong memories.

*Allison,
May your plate always
overflow with all of
your favorite things!
Jessica C. Williams*

JESSICA C. WILLIAMS

SAVVY FRIENDS
PRESS

ISBN 978-1-7359357-0-6
Library of Congress Control Number: 2020920098

First Edition
Published by Savvy Friends Press, Los Angeles, CA
savvyfriendspress.com

Printed in the United States of America

Art direction & Design: Roseline Seng, Rose Line Design
Photography: Sofía Felguérez & Alejandro Monfort, The Photo Pot
Food Styling: Nicole Kruzick, Belly Food Style
Printing: Marina Graphic Center

Additional credits:
Photos: Background detail (page 7) by Greta Schölderle Møller on Unsplash
Jessica's headshot (page 88) by Aurelia Dumont Photography
Dinnerware: Heath Ceramics (Coupe Line)
Typeface: Atten New by Miles Newlyn

jessicacwilliams.com

For Sam

With heaping helpings
of happiness

3 DAYS

12 RECIPES

20 HOURS

You got this!

CONTENTS

Welcome, Friends

As we gathered around our communal dining table one fall evening, feasting with family and friends, our son declared, "Thanksgiving is my favorite holiday!" Even a decade later, I will never forget that moment, his shining, innocent eyes sparking a sudden revelation: it was my duty to pass along the ability to create a turkey dinner that would make any mother proud. How hard could that be?

Growing up in a third-generation Chinese American household in Hawai'i, rice featured prominently at every meal—Thanksgiving, Christmas, and Easter included. We celebrated every holiday, American and Chinese, with our extended family, piling paper plates high with a mashup of "local kine grindz" (island foods) alongside imported holiday traditions like turkey or ham. At the time, I didn't understand why anyone would prefer bland turkey, metallic tasting cranberry sauce, or green beans drowned in canned soup, when right next to it, I could choose my grandma's insanely delicious deep-fried oyster rolls wrapped in pork caul fat; my great aunt's addicting potstickers or freshly made crunchy sesame balls; or my cousin's Spam® musubi. And there was always rice. Lots of rice.

Then I met and married this architect from Michigan.

Forging a new life together in our adopted hometown of Venice, California, little suspecting my education was about to begin, I observed with fascination how his "haole" (Hawaiian for white or Caucasian) family celebrated with perfectly roasted turkey and homemade stuffing served on nice, real china plates. Over the years I discovered not only the steps, but many unspoken secrets of producing a traditional turkey dinner. That meant no oyster rolls, no Spam® musubi, no potstickers, no sesame balls, no rice, and definitely no paper plates—at least not on Thanksgiving.

In hindsight, if I had known how many turkeys I would roast, potatoes I would mash, and pies I would bake in the production of this book, it might never have happened. Blissfully unaware and never lacking for eager taste testers, I gradually amassed and documented the steps, time line, checklists, and of course, the time-tested recipes that keep our family coming back for seconds every year.

They say lightning never strikes twice. But recently it dawned on me that tackling a turkey dinner is not just a holiday tradition for us: it's a team sport. It's a way to coauthor and edit the story of our family, as we quietly cement our bonds over browning sausage and simmering cider. Home-cooked meals, served up with sides of love, laughter, and a sense of community, nourish both body and spirit. These are the real reasons to stuff a bird, feed the fortunate, and in the process, make lifelong memories.

Let's get chopping!

Jessica

Let's Do This!

At least 1–2 weeks before
your dinner, follow the steps below.
Skip this part at your peril.

Step 1
Review this Guide

Review this entire guide preferably one week to a month before you attempt it. I highly recommend a cup of coffee, a glass of wine, or both. (Not together, of course.)

Grab a pen, highlighter, and/or sticky notes to mark up this guide. (Yes, you're allowed to do that!) Why not convince a buddy to join you? Making this a two-person job does spread the joy.

Step 2
Visualize Success

Let's start with logistics. If you are not set up to entertain, here's your chance to get creative. Go ahead, call your mom or a buddy to brainstorm if that's easier than coming up with a plan on your own.

A few key questions to consider: Who will be the lucky ones to get invited over? What will you sit on? Remember, borrowing or buying chairs is allowed. If you want music, give some thought to a playlist. Instrumental music is a classic choice.

Now take a tip from pro athletes and visualize. Take a look at the menu and photos. Visualize sitting down at a beautifully set table, inhaling the aromas and savoring the items on the menu. Imagine each guest, hear the laughter, the lively conversations, and yes, the compliments. Take as much time as you need.

Step 3
Invite Guests

Now that you have your guest list, invite them in person or electronically, and ask them to arrive on or after 4 pm on the given day.

If guests ask what they can bring, you might suggest the following items. Some white or rosé wine is the easy button. Pies or desserts are another option. After all, can you ever have too much of a good thing? Perhaps those who garden can bring some flowers from their own yard. Bottom line, keep it simple, since turkey and all the trimmings will be the main event.

Step 4
Clear the Refrigerator

Determine the date of the closest weekend before your dinner. That weekend, make enough room in the fridge for an object slightly larger than a bowling ball, and free up a shelf or two.

Now...it's showtime, baby!

THE
Menu

MAIN EVENT
Roast Turkey
Sausage Stuffing
Turkey Gravy

SIDES & SIPS
Garlic Mashed Potatoes
Green Bean Casserole
Sweet Potato Soufflé
Cranberry Sauce
Spiced Apple Cider

SWEET ENDINGS
Pumpkin Pie
Bourbon Pecan Pie
Whipped Cream

Countdown to Turkey Day

What to Do When

9 am
Review checklists and take stock
Clear the refrigerator
Remind guests

11 am
Go grocery shopping
(or order groceries)

3 pm
Take the rest of the day off

5 pm
Cranberry Sauce
Pie Crust

6 pm
Pumpkin Pie
Bourbon Pecan Pie

8:30 pm
Get pies in the oven
Plan tablescape (optional)

11 pm
Cover and refrigerate pies

SUNDAY

WEDNESDAY

9:30 am
Coffee, please

10 am
Sweet Potato Soufflé (prep, part 1)
Sausage Stuffing
Roast Turkey

1 pm
Turkey should be in the oven!
Whipped Cream (prep)
Green Bean Casserole (prep)

1:30 pm
Baste the turkey
Sweet Potato Soufflé (prep, part 2)

2:30 pm
Baste the turkey
Garlic Mashed Potatoes (prep)

3:30 pm
Baste the turkey
Spiced Apple Cider
Set the table
Serve beverages
Watch turkey carving videos

4 pm
*For 14-pound turkey, begin testing
for doneness.*
Green Bean Casserole (heat)
Sweet Potato Soufflé (heat)
Garlic Mashed Potatoes (boil and mash)
Sausage Stuffing (heat)
Turkey Gravy

4:30 pm
*For 15-pound turkey, begin testing
for doneness and adjust dinner time
accordingly.*
Serve side dishes
Carve and serve turkey
Light candles (optional)

5 pm
Let the feast begin!

5:30 pm
Pumpkin Pie
Bourbon Pecan Pie
Whipped Cream

6 pm
Ready, set, relax!

THURSDAY

Why bother?

I know this isn't easy. In fact you might rather walk on hot coals. If I could look inside your head, I might hear something like...

What are the benefits of cooking a whole turkey dinner?

You might have guessed some of the benefits already—eating, for one. People invariably find something on the spread they like, mostly because one helping of these dishes may contain enough fat or sugar for an entire day. But it's about more than just eating. Turkey dinners are about celebration. Now is not the time to get into the history of feasting, but a few words come to mind—laughter for one, and community, and love. If a turkey dinner equals laughter plus community plus love, what other reason do you need?

My kitchen is pretty small—I have limited counter space and pans, some of the burners on my stove don't work, and my oven isn't big enough for a turkey.

You, my friend, have serious issues—deal-breaker issues, in fact. There are ways to remedy these things, of course, like buying a disposable roasting pan or dropping a grand on a new oven. But if you aren't willing or able to remedy your equipment situation, your best bet would be to find a relative, friend, or even an acquaintance who has a suitable kitchen and equipment and offer to purchase the food and cook there (and clean up, of course). Who doesn't love the aroma of turkey? Since the host would get a free meal, it's hard to imagine anyone foolhardy enough to turn down your magnanimous offer.

SUNDAY

(6 hours)

The countdown to Turkey Day begins!

You will need this book, a pen or pencil, highlighter, and possibly an extra large coffee or tea. If you prefer, you could do these steps on Saturday instead of Sunday.

Turn the page for step-by-step instructions on getting ready for the big event, including some pretty pictures of the cooking equipment, baking supplies, serving essentials, and ingredients you'll need.

Note that even a small turkey will easily feed 12 or more guests at a pound per person. The side dish recipes will generally feed up to 8 people. Depending how many people you're expecting, double the side dish recipes for additional guests. For fewer guests, savor the leftovers or feed a fortunate friend or neighbor!

9 am

Go to the page marked **Let's Do This!** and make sure you have completed all of the steps.

Review the cooking equipment, baking supplies, and ingredients needed on the next few pages.

Then go to the **Checklists** section at the back. Using the **Cooking Equipment** and **Serving Essentials** checklists, mark off what you have and then substitute, borrow, or buy needed items—disposable versions will work too.

11 am

Before venturing out to your favorite grocery store, check off the items on the **Shopping List** that you already have.

Clear out your refrigerator and place a baking pan with a lip on it on a shelf where you will place the turkey to avoid leakage. DO NOT SKIP THIS STEP.

2 pm

Whew!
Take the rest of the day off.

TURKEY SAVVY

SHOPPING LIST

Organ... led whenever possible

BREAD / CANS / JARS
- ○ Bread, 2 loaves (1 white and 1 wheat, or both wheat)
- ○ Cream of Mushroom soup, 1 can (10.5-ounce)
- ○ French fried onions, 1 container (6-ounce)
- ○ Pumpkin, 1 can (15-ounce)

BAKING
- ○ Condensed milk, 1 can (12-ounce or 14-ounce)
- ○ Agave syrup, 1 cup
- ○ Flour, 6 cups—for pie crust, gravy thickener (alternative: 2-pack pre-made pie crusts)
- ○ Olive oil (EVOO preferred)
- ○ Maple syrup, ½ cup
- ○ Pecans, chopped, 3 cups (24 ounces)
- ○ Pecans, halves, 1 cup (8 ounces = about 60 halves)
- ○ Sugar, light or dark brown, 4 cups
- ○ Sugar, confectioners, ¼ cup
- ○ Vanilla, 1½ teaspoons
- ○ Walnuts, chopped, ½ cup (4 ounce)
- ○ Optional: Bourbon, ¼ cup

SPICES / GARNISH
- ○ Cinnamon, 4–6 sticks
- ○ Pepper, ground
- ○ Pumpkin pie spice or 1–2 teaspoons of these ground spices:
  - • Allspice
  - • Cinnamon
  - • Cloves

- ○ Sage, ... garnish)
- ○ Sea Sal... ...th)
- ○ Thyme, dri...
- ○ Optional: Pad...

PRODUCE
- ○ Apple, 1 (Fuji Gala, or b...
- ○ Celery, 2 bunches or b...
- ○ Cranberries, 1–2 bags (o... or two 8-ounce)
- ○ Garlic, 4 cloves
- ○ Green beans, 1 pound
- ○ Herbs, fresh 1 bunch each (dried ... acceptable)
  - • Rosemary
  - • Sage
  - • Thyme
- ○ Onions, 2 yellow
- ○ Orange, 1 navel
- ○ Potatoes, 6–8 med... Sweet potatoes,...

DAIRY
- ○ Milk, ½ cu...
- ○ Butter, ...
- ○ Ched... (4 o...
- ○ S...

COOKING EQUIPMENT

Wooden
Spoon

Metal
Spatula

Can
Opener

Small, Medium,
and Large Pots

Metal
Pins

Cooking
Thermometer

Vegetable
Peeler

Potato
Masher

Roasting Pan
and Rack

Kitchen
Shears

Cast Iron
Skillets

Colander

Electiric
Mixer

Vegetable
Peeler

Chopping Board

Carving
Fork

Chef's
Knife

Carving
Knife

Bread
Knife

Paring
Knife

Pastry
Brush

Wire
Whisk

Turkey
Baster

Pie Pan
(disposable)

Dry measuring
Cups

Loaf Pan

Pizza Pan

Pie Pan

Dried
Beans

Rubber
Spatulas

Wire
Cookie
Rack

24

Liquid Measuring
Cup

Mixing
Bowls

Measuring
Spoons

Wooden
Spoon

Rolling Pin

Cookie Sheet

Rubber
Spatula

Wooden
Spatula

25

SERVING ESSENTIALS

Large Serving
Platter

Trivets

Medium
Ladle

Tongs

Pie Spatula

Metal
Spatula

Metal
Spatula

Small
Ladle

Medium
Ladle

Small
Bowl

Large Serving
Spoon

Large Serving
Bowls

Dish Towel

27

Whipping
Cream

Eggs

Bread
(sliced)

Canned
Pumpkin

Celery

Rosemary

Thyme

Sage

French
Fried
Onions

Rosemary
(dried)

Thyme
(dried)

Sage
(dried)

Green
Beans

Pumpkin
Pie Spice

Pecans
(whole)

Pecans
(chopped)

Cinnamon
Sticks

Walnuts
(chopped)

Flour

Milk

Pork
Sausage

Lemon

Garlic

Sweet
Potato

Sour Cream

Turkey

TURKEY
RAISED WITHOUT ANTIBIOTICS
FED A VEGETARIAN DIET
NO PRESERVATIVES
GLUTEN FREE

Cranberries

Potato

Cream of Mushroom Soup

Orange

Campbell's
CONDENSED
GREAT FOR COOKING
Cream of
Mushroom
SOUP

Bourbon

Cheddar Cheese

Apple

Marshmallows

Onion

Powdered Sugar

White Sugar

Brown Sugar

Pepper

Sea Salt

Vanilla

Olive Oil

Condensed Milk

Butter

Maple Syrup

Agave Syrup

Apple Cider

Real talk

If you still have doubts, you're not alone.

Honestly, I'm afraid I'll fail—namely, the food won't look or taste good; my guests and I will be disappointed and say, 'Remember last year;' and I'll be a social reject.

There is always the possibility, despite following this guide to the letter, that something will go wrong, as things sometimes do. Ask yourself, if that were to happen: Will it kill me? Will my picture appear on the front page of the New York Times with the caption: "FAILURE"? Will my guests never speak to me ever again? No, I didn't think so. When the time comes to pull on your big-boy or big-girl pants and cook a turkey, YES you might fail. But you know what? The secret grown-ups know is this: Failure is not fatal! In fact, a fail can be your greatest teacher.

I don't want to be judged by my in-laws or guests—if I can't pull it off, I'll look bad.

Even though this guide is designed help you pull off a turkey dinner successfully and avoid this outcome, you still might want to consider why social disapproval is so important to you. I hate to be the bearer of bad news, but if someone is going to judge you for how well you make a turkey, well...see where I'm going with this? I'm not saying they have to love it or eat food that's not to their taste. But turkey dinners are more than just food. They're about family, friends, laughter—and about learning. Maybe, just maybe, a turkey dinner can show you who belongs in your life and who does not. Food for thought, isn't it?

WEDNESDAY

It's Turkey Dinner Eve!

Unless you have the day off from work, you will do this in the
evening. If you're a morning person, you could potentially
tack some or all of this on to Thursday morning, bearing in mind
that this will make for a long day on your feet.

I suggest spreading the joy over several days for several reasons.
Even if you have two ovens and could cook everything at
once, you still have to plan ahead. Most people probably aren't
used to standing and cooking for 10 hours straight, so this
breaks things up. Finally, it's always safer to allow some wiggle
room for the unexpected. Like insurance, if you have it you
probably won't need it, but if you don't, something unforeseen is
almost guaranteed to pop up and really throw the schedule off.

5pm

We'll start out nice and easy with homemade Cranberry Sauce. There are 3 required ingredients and 2 optional ingredients.

You're going to crush this!

CRANBERRY SAUCE

The most common response I got whenever I told friends I was going to make cranberries from scratch was, "It's really hard, you know." I'll let you be the judge of that once you've given this recipe a try.

**MAKES
ABOUT 2 CUPS**

1 cup water

1 cup sugar, white or brown (any type will work)

3 cups cranberries (12 ounces)

Optional

1 orange wedge

1 cinnamon stick

—

Equipment/Supplies

Small pot (4 cups)

Liquid measuring cup, glass

Dry measuring cups

Colander (or bowl)

Tablespoon

Food storage container (2-cup), preferably glass or ceramic

1. Add to a small pot and bring to a boil on High, stirring to combine:
    1 cup water
    1 cup sugar, white or brown (any type will work)

2. Rinse in a colander or bowl and discard any that are mushy or discolored:
    3 cups cranberries (12 ounces)
    Tip: Check labels as cranberries come in 8-ounce, 12-ounce, or 16-ounce bags. If fresh are not available, look for frozen ones.

3. When sugar has dissolved, add cranberries to pot. For a firmer cranberry jelly, add extra sugar. Less sugar results in a more tart and liquidy cranberry sauce.

4. If using, squeeze wedge over the cranberries and drop into the pot:
    1 orange wedge (optional)
    1 cinnamon stick (optional)

5. Turn heat to Medium and simmer for 10–15 minutes or longer, depending on the firmness of the berries, stirring occasionally. If your burners run hot, you may wish to use Medium Low.

6. When most of the berries have burst and you can easily break them against the side of the pot, they are done.

7. Pour into a storage container and allow to cool. (I like to leave the cinnamon stick and orange wedge in, but you may also remove them.)

8. Cover and refrigerate until ready to serve, preferably overnight.

5:30pm

You're 30 minutes in and you've completed
your first dish! Now let's move on to
the pie crust with 4 ingredients, if you don't
count ice.

Making a pie crust is a 3-part process: mix the
ingredients and refrigerate the dough for
at least 20 minutes; roll out the dough; and
prebake the crust. All of these steps can
be done in advance. While the dough is chilling
(literally) and prebaking, get a head start
on the pie fillings.

PIE CRUST

I learned to make a decent pie crust in the 8th grade in Home Economics class. It's a life skill that has been a great source of satisfaction. When people can't believe you made the crust yourself from scratch, it's a great feeling! However, premade pie crusts are an acceptable compromise if you prefer not to tackle this your first time out.

**MAKES
2 PIE CRUSTS**

About 1 cup cold water

3–4 ice cubes

1 cup butter, salted or unsalted (2 sticks)

2 ½ cups flour, plus ½ cup or more for rolling

1 teaspoon salt

MAKE DOUGH

1. Tear two wax paper rectangles about as long as your forearm and set aside. These will be used to wrap the dough.

2. In a cup or mug, add:
   About 1 cup cold water
   3–4 ice cubes

3. Remove from refrigerator and cut into 16 pieces:
   1 cup butter, salted or unsalted (2 sticks)
   Tip: Slice a stick in half lengthwise, then make 8 cuts crosswise—voilà, 16 pieces! Save the empty butter wrappers to butter the pie pans.

4. Measure the following into a mixing bowl:
   2 ½ cups flour
   1 teaspoon salt

5. Using the fork, begin to combine and "cut in" the butter. Your goal is to have a mixture that looks like small, uniform bread crumbs.

6. Rotate the bowl with one hand and use the fork in your other hand to press the tines through the butter. Periodically use a butter knife to scrape batter off the fork.

7. When the mixture looks like crumbs, stir with a wooden spoon or rubber spatula while sprinkling in cold water. (I use about 8 tablespoons of water, but you might need more or less.)

8. Dough should cling to the side of the bowl and form a ball. With clean hands, split dough in half, make two balls, and flatten them into thick disks.

Equipment/Supplies

Wax paper

Cup or mug

Mixing bowl

Dry measuring cups

Measuring spoons

Fork, butter knife, tablespoon

Wooden spoon or rubber spatula

Large chopping board or clean counter

Rolling pin (substitute: straight sided drinking glass, food safe roller)

2 pie pans (8-inch)

Parchment paper or aluminum foil

Pie weights or uncooked dried beans (substitute: uncooked rice, pot that fits inside the pie pan)

Oven mitts

Optional

2 wire cooling racks

9. Wrap each disk in wax paper and refrigerate for 30 minutes.

   NOTE: BEGIN MAKING THE PUMPKIN PIE AND BOURBON PECAN PIE FILLINGS NOW

ROLL OUT DOUGH (30 MINUTES LATER)

10. Butter 2 pie pans with the empty butter wrappers or a dab of butter on a piece of waxed paper. You may have to wash your hands in between some of the steps.

11. Sprinkle on a clean chopping board or counter: **½ cup flour or more**

12. Remove dough from the refrigerator, unwrap the disks, and place one disk on the floured board or counter. Rub some flour on a rolling pin. If the dough is hard to roll, wait until it softens.

13. Roll the disk into a flattened circle. To get a round shape, either change the direction of the rolling pin or pick up the dough and turn it 180 degrees periodically. If the dough sticks to the board, add more flour.

14. When the disk is about 2 inches larger than a pie pan placed upside down on the dough, put some flour on your hands and fold the circle loosely in half, then in quarters, to make a triangular piece of dough. Handle dough as little as possible, as overhandling can make the dough tough and chewy.

15. Place a dough triangle with the middle point at the center of the greased pie pan. Unfold the dough to fit the pie pan. If the shape is uneven, tear or cut pieces to fit the pie pan and press into place.

16. Trim overhanging edge so pastry is even with edge. Press any extra dough into thin parts of the crust or anywhere in the middle of the crust.

17. Use a fork to prick holes in the bottom and sides of the crust. You should have about 10 fork marks.

18. Press the fork tines around the edge of the pie crust to flatten or "fork" it.

19. Repeat with the second piece of dough.

PREBAKE CRUST (PART 1)

20. Preheat oven to 425 degrees F.

21. Tear two pieces of parchment paper or aluminum foil large enough to fit inside each crust.

22. Butter one side of the parchment or foil with an empty butter wrapper or wax paper.

23. Place parchment or foil butter side down, shaping it to the crust.

24. Weight the crust by pouring in either pie weights, dried beans, or rice. You can also place another pie pan or pot that fits inside the crust on top of the parchment or foil. Tip: If using rice or beans, store for future use or discard afterward.

25. Bake 10 minutes and remove from the oven.

PREBAKE CRUST (PART 2)

26. Turn oven down to 350 degrees F.

27. Remove weights and parchment or foil.

28. Bake another 10 minutes until crust browns. If the crust is not as browned as you like, brush some milk on it, then place back in the oven for a few more minutes.

29. Remove and cool, on a rack if possible, until ready to fill.

6pm

Next up: Pumpkin Pie filling with 7 ingredients.
Sure you could roast and mash a pumpkin,
but trust me on this, try the canned stuff and
thank me later.

While waiting for the pie crusts to prebake,
and when finished with the Pumpkin Pie filling,
move on to the Bourbon Pecan Pie filling.

PUMPKIN PIE

This is the "obligatory" but always welcome Thanksgiving dessert.
For an extra nice touch, make your own DIY Pumpkin Spice Mix!
Make a day ahead unless you have two ovens and plan ahead to get
both pies in the oven at the same time.

**MAKES
6–8 SERVINGS**

3 eggs, slightly beaten

1 can pumpkin (15-ounce)

1 can condensed milk
(14-ounce)

¾ cup brown sugar

½ teaspoon salt

2 teaspoons pumpkin
pie spice

1 pie crust

Note: If using premade
pie crusts, you may need
two pie crusts for this
recipe if they are shallow.

DIY Pumpkin Spice Mix

¼ teaspoon allspice

1 teaspoon cinnamon

¼ teaspoon cloves

¼ teaspoon ginger

¼ teaspoon nutmeg

1. Preheat oven to 400 degrees F. Ensure that oven racks
   are set up to bake both pies at once. Plan ahead to
   bake both pumpkin and pecan pies together. If you are
   prebaking the pie crusts while making the pie fillings,
   the oven may already be warm.

2. Break into mixing bowl and beat with a wire whisk or
   fork until frothy:
   3 eggs, slightly beaten

3. Open the containers and use a rubber spatula to scrape
   into the mixing bowl:
   1 can pumpkin (15-ounce)
   1 can condensed milk (14-ounce)
   Tip: You could bake and mash your own pumpkin, but canned
   pumpkin works well. Use plain canned pumpkin, not "pumpkin
   pie mix."

4. Add dry ingredients and whisk to combine:
   ¾ cup brown sugar
   ½ teaspoon salt
   2 teaspoons pumpkin pie spice
   Tip: Buy premixed spices or if feeling ambitious and have the
   ingredients, make the DIY Pumpkin Spice Mix.

5. If you have not yet rolled out and prebaked the pie crust,
   return to the Pie Crust recipe and complete those steps.
   If using premade crusts, skip this step.

6. Place prebaked crust(s) on a pizza pan or cookie sheet.

7. Pour filling into pie crust, scraping the bowl with the
   rubber spatula.

8. Carefully transfer pizza pan or cookie sheet to oven rack,
   making sure not to spill filling.

Equipment/Supplies

Mixing bowl

Can opener

Dry measuring cups

Measuring spoons

Wire whisk or fork

Rubber spatula

Pizza pan or cookie sheet

Oven mitts

Wire rack

Aluminum foil

9. Bake for 45–50 minutes.

Tip: Place both pies in the oven at the same time, if possible.

10. Begin testing for doneness at 45 minutes. Insert a butter knife in the center. When it comes out clean, the filling has set. If not, filling will cling to the knife. If so, leave in the oven, testing every 5 minutes until done.

11. Remove from oven and cool, preferably on a wire rack.

12. Cover with foil and refrigerate. If still warm when placing in the refrigerator, place a trivet underneath the pie.

Is it really worth it?

You'll only know if you give it a try.

How long will this take and how much will it cost?

Plan to commit approximately 20 hours (yes, that's half a work week), spread out over three days. Enjoy the journey, not just the destination! As for the price tag, it depends on what you have already, food prices, and quantities. You might spend $20 or more per person, but fortunately, you will likely have enough leftovers to feed a family of four for several days afterward.

What if I don't have all the utensils or ingredients I need? Can I substitute pre-made items?

You can get some disposable items, but here's your big chance to get creative and substitute or borrow equivalent tools. Or look at it as a chance to invest in stocking up your kitchen—not to mention a fine opportunity for some "retail therapy." You can always substitute premade, frozen or canned equivalents, but I suggest you try it from scratch at least once. Then you can tell me why your way saves time and tastes better.

7pm

Time to up your game. There are 10 ingredients in Bourbon Pecan Pie. Are you up for the challenge?

Pie crusts should be prebaking by now. Plan ahead to get both pies in the oven at the same time.

8:30pm

When the pie crusts come out of the oven, be ready to fill them and get them in the oven together. It's not time to kick back just yet. Chill some water, iron napkins, and plan out the tablescape, if you're so inclined.

11pm

Cover and refrigerate pies. Bedtime!

BOURBON PECAN PIE

A lush and impressive way to conclude the day's festivities.
Notice that agave syrup replaces the traditional corn syrup. May be
made without bourbon if desired.

**MAKES
6–8 SERVINGS**

6 tablespoons butter,
salted or unsalted
(¾ stick of butter)

1 cup pecans, halves
(60 pieces)

3 eggs, slightly beaten

1 ¼ cup brown sugar

¼ teaspoon salt

1 teaspoon vanilla

¾ cup agave syrup

1 cup pecans, chopped

1 pie crust

Optional

¼ cup bourbon

Note: If using premade pie
crusts, you may need two
pie crusts for this recipe if
they are shallow.

1. Preheat oven to 400 degrees F. Ensure that oven racks
   are set up to bake both pies at once. Plan ahead to
   bake both pumpkin and pecan pies together. If you are
   prebaking the pie crusts while making the pie fillings,
   the oven may already be warm.

2. Use tablespoon markings on the wrapper (if available) to
   cut off the correct amount and place in a small pot:
   6 tablespoons butter, salted or unsalted (¾ stick of butter)

3. Melt and swirl occasionally, until butter foams, bubbles,
   and turns light golden brown, about 2 minutes.
   Do not allow to burn. Set aside to cool.

4. Pick out 60 pieces for the topping, the most perfect ones
   you can find:
   1 cup pecans, halves (60 pieces)

5. Break into mixing bowl and beat with a wire whisk or fork
   until frothy:
   3 eggs, slightly beaten

6. Add the following ingredients one at a time, blending each
   separately with the wire whisk or fork:
   1 ¼ cup brown sugar
   ¼ teaspoon salt
   1 teaspoon vanilla
   ¾ cup agave syrup

7. Using the rubber spatula, fold in the cooled butter, plus the
   following:
   1 cup pecans, chopped
   ¼ cup bourbon (optional)

8. If you have not yet rolled out and prebaked the pie crust,
   return to the Pie Crust recipe and complete those steps. If
   using premade crusts, skip this step.

Equipment/Supplies

Small pot (4-cup)

Mixing bowl

Wire whisk or fork

Dry measuring cups

Measuring spoons

Liquid measuring cup, glass

Rubber spatula

Pizza pan or cookie sheet

Oven mitts

Wire rack

Aluminum foil

9. Place prebaked crust(s) on a pizza pan or cookie sheet.

10. Pour filling into pie crust, scraping the bowl with the rubber spatula.

11. Arrange 60 pecan halves on top of the pie in a circular pattern, starting with the outer ring. You should have about 30 pecans in the outer ring, 20 in the middle ring, and 10 in the inner ring.

12. Carefully transfer pizza pan or cookie sheet to oven rack, making sure not to spill filling.

13. Bake for 45–50 minutes.
Tip: Place both pies in the oven at the same time, if possible.

14. Begin testing for doneness at 45 minutes. Insert a butter knife in the center. When it comes out clean, the filling has set. If not, filling will cling to the knife. If so, leave in the oven, testing every 5 minutes until done.

15. Remove from oven and cool, preferably on a wire rack.

16. Cover with foil and refrigerate. If still warm when placing in the refrigerator, place a trivet underneath the pie.

Counting Calories?
Not today.

Where are the dinner rolls and salad?

Like some households, we've cut back our wheat consumption. If you must have these, commercial varieties are readily available. Like pies and flowers, dinner rolls are a good thing to suggest when guests say, "What can I bring?" For some reason, salad has been a tough sell.

Pro Tip: Save the greens for the day after.

Why haven't you included calorie counts?

Seriously. May I suggest taking the day off from counting calories? If you absolutely must, online calorie counters are readily available. Besides, it's not just the quantity of calories consumed, but the quality. Processed food may be convenient, but by cooking at home, you can control the ingredients and preparation methods, ending up with a much healthier result.

Should I or shouldn't I?

It's not too late for takeout, but just remember, as legendary scientist Albert Einstein once said, "A person who never made a mistake never tried anything new." It's a great day for an Einstein moment!

It's just so daunting, especially when I didn't grow up making these dishes— we either went to someone's house or bought pre-made food.

Yes. It is daunting. Next? No really, I get it, I really do. This is one of those How to Adult lessons that those of us who grew up in a hyphenated household (Asian-American, Latin-American, etc.) completely missed. In some cultures, rice goes with everything— I'm looking at you, cranberry sauce! You are correct, cooking a turkey dinner is a serious investment of time, energy, and money. Going into it, you'll increase your chances of success if you are clear on the reasons you're expending the effort. Either you want to cook a turkey or you don't. If you do, this guide will make it easy. If you don't, there's always takeout.

What if I want to eat this but have no interest in going through all the steps?

Well, that's honest. This is where your powers of persuasion come in. Here's my suggestion: (1) Find a friend who likes to cook. (2) Gift them this guide. (3) Offer to go shopping with them and either split the cost or pay for the ingredients. (4) To further sweeten the deal, you can always offer to do the dishes. Forever. Done!

THURSDAY

And now, it's showtime.

Break out the apron and comfy shoes. Start the day with a shower
and breakfast. A double shot cappuccino right about now is not
a bad idea. In fact, you might want to keep that coffee pot fired up
and put on some tunes if either of those things appeal to you.

Turkey and the trimmings are best as a team sport. The saying
"Many hands make light work" was tailor made for this event.
Pro tip: If you can get others to assist—whether family, friends,
honored guests, or what I call mystery guests: people you've
never met who came with a friend—they can begin working on
other recipes in parallel, which will make the work go faster.

On your mark...get set...COOK!

10am

Before you start the stuffing, begin roasting the sweet potatoes (see Sweet Potato Soufflé). This should take about an hour.

In the meantime, we'll start the day with the most complex recipe containing the most steps and ingredients: Sausage Stuffing.

SAUSAGE STUFFING

This is the second-most labor-intensive part after the turkey, with the most ingredients and many steps. Fortunately, it's the first thing you tackle on Thursday when you're fresh.

**MAKES
16+ CUPS**
(enough for a 20-pound turkey)

2 cups butter, salted or unsalted (4 sticks)

2 pounds pork sausage (2 packages, 16 ounces each)

3 cups celery, chopped (1 bunch or package)

1 ½ cups onion, chopped (1 medium onion)

2 loaves bread (white and/ or wheat)

Olive oil for sautéing

½ cup walnuts, chopped

2 teaspoons salt

1 teaspoon pepper

3 teaspoons sage, dried (6 teaspoons fresh)

2 teaspoons thyme, dried (4 teaspoons fresh)

PREP WORK AREA

1. Wear an apron or "boro boros" (in Hawaiian Pidgin, worn out clothing) in case of greasy splatters.

2. Put out a medium size "rubbish bowl" or plastic bag for vegetable peels and wrappers.

3. Take out 1–2 large skillets, cast iron if you have them.

SAUSAGE OPERATION
If you have two or more people, the second person can start the vegetable and bread operations while the first is completing the sausage operation.

4. In the first skillet, melt on Low heat:
   ½ cup butter, salted or unsalted (1 stick)

5. Cut open packages and sauté in butter on Medium heat, using a wooden spoon to break into small, uniform chunks, stirring occasionally to brown evenly:
   2 pounds pork sausage (2 packages, 16 ounces each)

6. When the sausage is uniformly dark brown, scoop it into the large pot. Don't clean the skillet.

VEGETABLE OPERATION
If you have two or more people, a second person can chop the vegetables in parallel with the sausage operation.

7. If you only have one skillet, use it after emptying out the cooked sausage or use a second skillet if you have one to melt on Low heat:
   ½ cup butter, salted or unsalted (1 stick)

Equipment/Supplies

1–2 cast iron skillets, large if possible

Medium size bowl or plastic bag

Kitchen shears or scissors

Chopping board, large

Chef's knife

Bread knife or serrated steak knife

Mixing bowl

Wooden spoon

Dry measuring cups

Measuring spoons

Large pot or large bowl (ideally 16+ cups)

Mixing bowl

Glass bowl or baking pan (9 x 13 inch)

Large metal spoon

8. To prepare the celery, pull off individual stalks, wash, chop off and discard top and bottom ends. Using a chef's knife, slice lengthwise and dice into small (¼ to ½ inch) pieces. To get the pieces even smaller, rock the knife over the chopped pieces again.
3 cups celery, chopped (1 bunch or package)

9. To prepare the onion, peel, chop off and discard the stem (top) end, but leave the roots on. Using the chef's knife, place the flat end (top) down and slice in half starting at the root end. Lay the halves flat and cut into half rings, then slice crosswise to dice into small (¼ to ½ inch) pieces.
1 ½ cups onion, chopped (1 medium onion)

10. Place chopped vegetables in the skillet with butter and sauté, stirring occasionally.

11. When the onions are translucent, scoop vegetables into the large pot and combine with the sausage. Don't clean the skillet.

BREAD CUBE OPERATION
If you have two or more people, the second person can cube the bread after completing the vegetable operation.

12. If you have two skillets, melt one stick in each one on Low heat. If you have only one skillet, do this in two batches.
1 cup butter, salted or unsalted (2 sticks)

13. Take out 32 slices (2 slices equals about 1 cup of cubes):
2 loaves bread (white and/or wheat)

14. Using a bread knife and working in stacks of 3–4 slices, cut off the crusts. Then cut stacks of 3–4 slices of bread into cubes. Feel free to use the crusts if you wish.

15. Measure 8 cups of bread cubes into the skillet and toss cubes in butter and pan juices.
Tip: If you only have one skillet, repeat the process after you finish the first one.

16. Sauté over Medium heat until bread cubes begin to brown. If cubes look dry, drizzle with:
Olive oil for sautéing

17. Pour bread cubes into the pot with the sausage mixture and stir to coat the bread cubes evenly.

NUTS & SPICES OPERATION
If you have two or more people, the second person can chop the nuts after cubing the bread.

18. Measure onto a chopping board:
½ cup walnuts, chopped

19. Even if the package says, "chopped walnuts," chop them further to the consistency of a coarse "nut dust." Pour walnuts into the pot with the sausage and bread cubes.

20. Measure spices into a bowl or small plate:
2 teaspoons salt
1 teaspoon pepper
3 teaspoons sage, dried (6 teaspoons fresh)
2 teaspoons thyme, dried (4 teaspoons fresh)
Tip: When using fresh herbs, double the amount of the dried version.

21. Pour spices into the pot with the sausage and bread cubes. Use a wooden spoon or rubber spatula to combine all ingredients.

22. Using a large metal spoon, place several cups of stuffing into a mixing bowl. If you make the stuffing ahead of time, do this step right before you stuff the bird.

23. Place remaining stuffing in large glass bowl or baking pan, cover with foil, and refrigerate until ready to heat.

HEAT STUFFING (10 MINUTES BEFORE SERVING)

24. When the turkey comes out, preheat the oven to 350 degrees F. During or after baking the Green Bean Casserole, put the Sausage Stuffing in the oven for 10 minutes to reheat and brown the top. Spoon stuffing into a serving bowl. (I place the stuffing from inside and outside the bird into separate serving bowls.)

12pm

The stuffing should be ready or close to going into the bird.

1pm

Bird should be stuffed and in the oven no later than 1 pm. Set a timer to go off every 30 minutes to remind yourself to baste. However, if you miss a basting (or most of them), as long as you get in a few good bastings with the pan juices, you're fine.

ROAST TURKEY

This is it...your chance to cook the big bird. With over 30 steps, this is arguably the most complex operation. But with these tips, you can conceivably "hit it out of the park" on your first try. Note that this is much easier as a team sport. Two people is ideal—one to hold the turkey and the other to wrangle the stuffing. Alrighty, take a deep breath and as our gamer son would say, "Lezzz go!"

SERVES
1 POUND PER PERSON

1 turkey, 14–16 pounds (defrosted or fresh)

4–6 cups Sausage Stuffing or more

4 teaspoons salt

2 teaspoons pepper

½ cup olive oil

Optional

Sprigs of rosemary, sage, and/or thyme

TIPS
- Estimate 1 pound of turkey per person, more if you want leftovers. However, the smallest turkeys are still around 14 pounds.
- Buy frozen turkey a minimum of three days in advance and begin defrosting.
- This is much easier with two people!

PREP THE WORK AREA

1. Remove oven racks, leaving only the lowest rack. (I store them temporarily on top of the refrigerator.)

2. Don an apron and/or food safe gloves if desired.

3. Clean the kitchen sink with detergent. If needed, wash and dry the roasting pan and rack.

4. Set up the roasting pan and rack next to the sink. If you don't have a roasting rack, coarsely chop 2–3 onions or carrots and place them in the bottom of the roasting pan.

5. Place 6 clean metal pins on the counter.

6. Place a plastic bag in the sink for discarding the turkey wrapping and giblets.

7. Scoop into a bowl placed next to the sink:
   4–6 cups Sausage Stuffing or more

Equipment/Supplies

Kitchen shears or scissors

Plastic bag

Roasting pan (if using a disposable pan, use 2 pans together to make it easier to lift)

Roasting rack (substitute: use roughly chopped onions or carrots instead)

6 metal pins (substitute: kitchen twine)

Large serving spoon

Oven mitts

Turkey baster

Meat thermometer

Chopping board, large

Carving knife

Carving fork

Large serving platter

Serving fork or tongs

Aluminum foil and/or large resealable bag

Optional

Apron

Food safe gloves

Pastry brush

STUFF THE BIRD

After the prep work Is done, I can stuff the bird alone in about 17 minutes. However, if you have two people, it goes even faster as one can hold the bird while the other can stuff it.

WARNING: To avoid transferring harmful bacteria, don't allow raw turkey juices to touch anything that will be eaten, such as stuffing that doesn't fit inside the turkey. Be sure to wash and dry your hands and utensils like the kitchen shears after touching raw turkey.

8. Place in the sink:
   1 turkey, 14–16 pounds (defrosted or fresh)

9. Cut open the bag with kitchen shears and remove wrapping and giblets from the turkey cavity. Some turkeys do not come with giblets (extra parts of the turkey which are not always eaten). If desired, keep the neck and heart, but discard liver and gizzards in the plastic bag.
   Tip: If your turkey isn't fully thawed, there may be chunks of ice in the cavity. Remove the ice before stuffing. If needed, run water into the cavity to loosen the ice.

10. If you don't have metal pins, skip ahead to step 14 to stuff the main cavity only.

11. If you have metal pins, place the bird upright in the sink with the smaller neck cavity facing up.

12. Holding the bird upright with the neck cavity open, use your other hand to spoon stuffing into the back cavity. If you have a second person, one can hold the turkey while the other one scoops the stuffing inside. Don't pack the stuffing in too tightly, as it will expand during cooking.

13. Use 1–2 metal pins to "sew" the skin in place over the stuffing.

14. Flip the turkey so that the larger main cavity faces up.

15. Holding the bird upright with the main cavity open, use your other hand to spoon stuffing into the back cavity. If you have a second person, one can hold the turkey while

the other one scoops the stuffing inside. Don't pack the stuffing in too tightly, as it will expand during cooking. Tip: If you need more stuffing, use a second, clean spoon to transfer it to the bowl to avoid contamination with raw turkey juices.

16. Use 2–4 metal pins to "sew" the skin in place over the stuffing. If you don't have pins, you can also use food safe kitchen twine to tie the legs loosely together.

17. Discard any leftover stuffing that doesn't fit inside the turkey.

18. Place the turkey, breast side up, on the roasting rack (or on top of the chopped onions or carrots). If using the neck and/or heart, place them next to the turkey or on top of the stuffing.

19. Drizzle the turkey with:
    4 teaspoons salt
    2 teaspoons pepper
    ½ cup olive oil

20. Use your hands or a pastry brush to distribute oil and seasonings evenly all over the turkey.

ROAST THE BIRD (15 MINUTES PER POUND)
Get the turkey in the oven no later than 1 pm.

21. Turn the oven to 325 degrees F, ideally using the convection setting. Estimated cooking times:
    - 14 pound turkey = 3.5 hours
    - 15 pound or more turkey = 3.75 hours

22. Place the bird on the lowest rack.

23. Set the turkey baster on a plate next to the oven.

24. Set a timer (phone timer is fine) for basting every 30 minutes or so with pan juices.

NOTE: WHILE THE TURKEY IS ROASTING, TAKE THE OPPORTUNITY TO SIT DOWN AND POSSIBLY REVIEW SOME TURKEY CARVING VIDEOS OR ARTICLES.

25. To baste, open the oven and with an oven mitt, pull the rack out halfway.

26. Carefully grab one side of the roasting pan and tip it so that the pan juices collect on one side.

27. With your other hand, place the tip of the turkey baster in the pan juices and squeeze to collect juices, then coat the turkey skin. Repeat several times to coat the entire turkey.

    - If juices run low, add a cup of water.
    - If you wish, rotate the turkey after basting to brown it evenly.
    - If the breast or legs begin to brown too quickly, cover those pieces with a piece of foil (also called "tenting"). Remove the foil about 15 minutes before the turkey is done.

    Tip: Don't stress out if you miss a basting. I usually end up basting it only twice.

NOTE: BEGIN WORKING ON THE OTHER RECIPES AND TASKS NOW

TEST FOR DONENESS

28. For a 14 pound bird, start testing around 4 pm or 15 minutes later for every pound in weight. To test for doneness, place a meat thermometer between the breast and thigh, not in the drumstick.

    Tip: Oven temperatures vary, so pay attention to how it smells— when it smells "done," you should begin checking it.

NOTE: TURKEY IS DONE WHEN A MEAT THERMOMETER REACHES AT LEAST 175 DEGREES F.

CARVE THE BIRD

29. Place a chopping board, ideally with a rim to catch pan juices, on top of a kitchen towel on the counter. This will stabilize it while carving.

30. Set out a carving knife and fork.

31. When the turkey is done, remove turkey from the oven and transfer to the chopping board.

32. Allow turkey to rest for 20 minutes before carving.

33. Carve the turkey. Hopefully, you had a chance to view a turkey carving video or article. You may want to:
    - Remove the legs and wings first.
    - Remove the breast.
    - Carve the pieces individually.

    Tip: If you have 6 guests or less, cut up only half the turkey to keep the meat from drying out.

34. Arrange carved turkey slices and pieces on a serving platter. If desired, garnish with:
    Sprigs of rosemary, sage, or thyme (optional)

35. Cover and refrigerate any remaining turkey.

AFTER DINNER

36. Place leftover bones and carcass in a resealable bag to make stock or soup and freeze if you don't plan to use the bones immediately.

1pm

With the turkey in the oven, it's time to start prepping sides. Breaks are allowed and hydration is encouraged too!

Place a clean, dry metal bowl and mixing beaters or a wire whisk in your newly cleared refrigerator. Remove a block of butter for the Sweet Potato Soufflé. Then prepare the Green Bean Casserole—put it in a dish that can go from oven to table, like a 9 x 13 inch baking dish or a cast iron skillet.

GREEN BEAN CASSEROLE

We refer to this recipe as "Green Beans Marcelyn," in honor of a dear Osage friend from Oklahoma who introduced me to this traditional Thanksgiving classic. We like to use fresh green beans, but you can substitute 4 cups frozen or canned green beans in a pinch.

**MAKES
6–8 SERVINGS**

1 pound green beans (16 ounces)

About 6 dashes of salt

¼ teaspoon salt

¼ teaspoon pepper

1 can Cream of Mushroom Soup (10.5-ounce)

½ cup sour cream

½ cup cheddar cheese, shredded

1 can french fried onions (6-ounce)

MAKE AHEAD

1. Rinse, snap off, and discard stem ends and any whole or parts that are soft from:
   1 pound green beans (16 ounces)

2. Place beans in a medium pot, fill with enough water to cover the beans, and shake in:
   About 6 dashes of salt

3. Bring pot to a boil and cook about 5 minutes, until beans are bright green and slightly tender. To test, pierce with a fork—you should feel a little give, but ideally, they should not be too soft.

4. Drain beans in a colander or lift out with a slotted spoon or tongs and place cooked beans in a 9 x 13 inch baking pan or cast-iron skillet.

5. Sprinkle with:
   ¼ teaspoon salt
   ¼ teaspoon pepper

6. Open containers and using a rubber spatula, scrape on top of the green beans:
   1 can Cream of Mushroom Soup (10.5-ounce)
   ½ cup sour cream

7. If using a block of cheese instead of pre-shredded cheese, grate with a box grater. Otherwise, skip to the next step.

8. Sprinkle on top of the green beans:
   ¼ cup cheddar cheese, shredded
   French fried onions (3 ounces)
   Tip: Remember to save half of the cheese and french fried onions for the topping.

Equipment/Supplies

Medium pot (8 cups)

Colander (substitute: slotted spoon, tongs)

Baking pan (9 x 13 inch) or cast-iron skillet

Can opener

Measuring spoons

Dry measuring cups

Wooden spoon

Oven mitts

Trivet (substitute: potholder, folded kitchen towel)

Optional

Box grater (if cheese is not pre-shredded)

9. Gently combine all ingredients together with a wooden spoon or rubber spatula.

10. Cover and refrigerate until ready to heat.

BAKE CASSEROLE
(30 MINUTES BEFORE SERVING)
Bake this at the same time as the Sweet Potato Soufflé. You will need to place a second rack in the oven.

11. When the turkey comes out of the oven, preheat oven to 350 degrees F.

12. Bake for 25 minutes or until hot and bubbling.

13. Remove from the oven but leave the oven on.

14. Stir the hot bean mixture.

15. Spread with a layer of cheese followed by a layer of onions:
¼ cup cheddar cheese, shredded
French fried onions (3 ounces)

16. Place back in oven and bake another 5 minutes at 350 degrees F until french fried onions are golden brown.
Tip: When serving, place on trivet or potholder as pan will be hot.

To stream or not to stream
How about some tips from a professional DJ?

Where do I start?

When deciding what music to play, consider the mood: Lively or subdued? Casual dinner party or formal ceremony? One host may like classical or jazz, another may prefer Motown. Ask around and compile a list of 10–15 songs people like. Then it's time to build a playlist from your own collection or use a premade one. Yes, like prebaked pie crusts, you can get a ready-made playlist these days. Even free services offer these, although you might want to test them to see if they include ads between songs.

Should I build or should I buy?

Now that you have an idea of the mood you want to create, let's get practical. Do you have access to a free or paid streaming music service? Will you be using recorded music from CDs or on a computer? If you already have a subscription to a music service, that's the logical solution. If not, go to a web browser and type "free music services" in the search bar to learn what is available. Make sure you have a decent Bluetooth speaker and adjust the volume to the activity. Happy listening!

1:30pm

Basting officially begins. Put that turkey baster to good use for once!

When you finish preparing the green beans, the sweet potatoes you roasted earlier should be cool enough to remove from their jackets and combine with the softened butter and other ingredients. You'll bake this when the turkey is removed from the oven.

SWEET POTATO SOUFFLÉ

After many years of skipping sweet potatoes, this recipe was a recent addition, thanks to another mom who made and brought this over when I was recovering from surgery. Highly recommend for recovering from anything!

**MAKES
6–8 SERVINGS**

5 sweet potatoes, medium

½ cup butter, at room temperature (1 stick)

Pinch of salt

1 ½ teaspoons vanilla

½ cup maple syrup

½ cup milk

2 eggs

½ teaspoon cinnamon

1 handful miniature marshmallows (or to taste)

1 handful whole or chopped pecans (or to taste)

ROAST SWEET POTATOES (PREP, PART 1)

If desired, these can be prepared a day or more ahead, wrapped in foil, and refrigerated.

1. Preheat oven to 350 degrees F.

2. Cover a cookie sheet with foil.

3. Wash and poke with a fork:
   5 sweet potatoes, medium

4. Place on foil-covered cookie sheet and bake about 1 hour.

5. Test for doneness by poking each potato with a fork. Potatoes are done when a fork slides easily through the thickest part of the largest potato.

ASSEMBLE SOUFFLÉ (PREP, PART 2)

6. Remove from refrigerator to soften:
   ½ cup butter, at room temperature (1 stick)

7. Cut sweet potatoes in half lengthwise (along the long side) and use a spoon to scrape the flesh into the mixing bowl. Place peels on the foil and wrap to discard.

8. With a potato masher, mash the potato flesh until smooth.

9. Add softened butter and mash to combine (saving the wrapper for the next step).

10. Use the empty butter wrapper or a dab of butter on a piece of waxed paper to grease your baking dish (square pan or loaf pan).

Equipment/Supplies

Cookie sheet

Aluminum foil

Fork, Tablespoon

Oven mitts

Mixing bowl

Chef's knife

Chopping board

Potato masher

Square pan (8-inch)
or loaf pan

Measuring spoons

Liquid measuring cup,
glass

Electric mixer or wire
whisk

Rubber spatula

Trivet (substitute:
potholder, folded kitchen
towel)

11. Add additional ingredients and combine with an electric mixer on Medium or a wire whisk:
Pinch of salt
1 ½ teaspoons vanilla
½ cup maple syrup
½ cup milk
2 eggs

12. Using a rubber spatula, scrape the mixture into the baking dish.

13. Sprinkle the souffle with toppings to taste:
½ teaspoon cinnamon
1 handful miniature marshmallows (or to taste)
1 handful whole or chopped pecans (or to taste)

BAKE SOUFFLÉ (40 MINUTES BEFORE SERVING)

Bake this at the same time as the Green Bean Casserole.
You will need to place a second rack in the oven.
When the Green Beans come out after 30 minutes, put in the Sausage Stuffing to reheat for 10 minutes.

14. When the turkey comes out, preheat the oven to 350 degrees F.

15. Bake about 40 minutes, until marshmallows are lightly browned.
Tip: When serving, place on trivet or potholder as pan will be hot.

If not now, when?

I think it's called "adulting."

First time cooking an entire turkey dinner for the whole family?

Learning to cook a turkey and all the trimmings has never been easier with all the great cooking videos and mobile apps available, not to mention the lovely guide you're reading. Just think, here's your chance to learn something new, eat well, and maybe impress family and friends in the process.

Alone at Thanksgiving this year?

If you're celebrating solo, scale back to a turkey breast and a few sides. (Cranberry Sauce, anyone?) Alternatively, roast an entire turkey and avoid cooking again for a week. And if you share some with a fortunate neighbor, you just may make a lifelong friend.

2:30pm

Another good time to baste!

When the sweet potatoes are tucked away in the refrigerator next to the Green Bean Casserole, get the potatoes peeled and ready to go as it gets closer to dinner.

GARLIC MASHED POTATOES

Growing up in Hawai'i, potatoes were a treat which we only seemed to have on special occasions. Like rice, this is the Swiss Army knife of sides. Use this recipe all year long with beef, pork, poultry, seafood, or vegetarian dishes.

MAKES
6–8 SERVINGS

8 red or 4 russet potatoes, medium

2 garlic cloves, unpeeled

¼ cup butter (½ block)

¼ cup heavy cream or milk

Salt and pepper

Optional

Butter, 1–2 tablespoons

Fresh ground pepper

Parsley, fresh or dried

MAKE AHEAD

1. Peel and use a paring knife to cut off bruises, eyes, and spots from:
   8 red or 4 russet potatoes, medium
   Tip: Do not use green potatoes as they contain solanine, which is toxic. However, you may be able to peel off the green part.

2. Cut peeled potatoes into uniform halves or quarters with a chef's knife.

3. Rinse and place potato pieces in a medium or large pot with:
   2 garlic cloves, unpeeled

4. Fill pot with water to cover potatoes.

HEAT AND MASH
(30 MINUTES BEFORE SERVING)
Do this while the Roast Turkey is resting and the Green Bean Casserole and Sweet Potato Soufflé are baking.

5. Bring water to a boil on High and boil 10–15 minutes.

6. Test with a fork. When the fork easily pierces the largest piece, they are done.

7. Remove from heat with potholders and pour off most of the water, leaving a little water on the bottom.

8. Remove garlic cloves. Cloves will be hot. Discard the skins and replace cloves in pot. (I prefer to cut off and discard the hard stem end of the garlic clove.)

Equipment/Supplies

Vegetable peeler

Paring knife

Chopping board

Chef's knife

Medium (8 cups) or
large pot (12 cups)

Oven mitts

Fork

Dish towel

Potato masher

Liquid measuring cup,
glass

Rubber spatula

9. Add to the pot:
    ¼ cup butter (½ block)
    ¼ cup heavy cream or milk
    Salt and pepper

10. Place the pot on a folded dishtowel on the counter.

11. Using a potato masher, mash all ingredients until the
    desired consistency is reached. If needed, add
    more cream, milk, or water.

12. Taste and adjust salt and/or pepper as needed.

13. Scrape into serving bowl with rubber spatula.

14. Garnish with desired toppings such as:
    Butter, 1–2 tablespoons (optional)
    Fresh ground pepper (optional)
    Parsley, fresh or dried (optional)

Love those leftovers

Most likely, you'll spend the next week recycling turkey into other dishes.

What's the best thing to do with leftovers?

Our family favorites include cold turkey sandwiches slathered with mayo and a grind of fresh pepper; hot open-faced turkey sandwiches, ideally on white bread, with hot gravy; turkey pot pie with homemade pie crust; hearty and comforting turkey wild rice soup; and the classic Cantonese jook (congee) using an entire turkey carcass! We sometimes have a Black Friday dinner with friends, pooling various versions of stuffing and sides—a fun way to get in some visiting and spread love, joy, and leftovers around. Pecan Pie, anyone?

What is Turkey Tetrazzini?

If you thought this was an Italian dish, you would be forgiven. However. you would also be wrong.

According to Wikipedia, although this dish is named after Luisa Tetrazzini, a 19th century Italian opera singer, it allegedly originated in San Francisco around 1908, where Tetrazzini had performed a few years earlier. Poultry, seafood, or vegetarian options are mixed with some combination of butter, cream, and cheese. Serve it as a pasta sauce or baked as a casserole. Buon appetito!

SETTING THE SCENE

If you have not yet done so, this would be a good time to get out the real dishes, glasses, and serving essentials. You might also want to watch some turkey carving videos.

By now, you know what I'm going to say about basting.

Get the Spiced Apple Cider going to fill your home with the most gorgeous fall bouquet of scents. If your kids like this as much as ours do, you might want to make some extra that you can chill for later.

SPICED APPLE CIDER

May be served hot or cold. A kid-friendly favorite, we always get an extra jug or two to double or scale up the amounts for more or larger servings. Substitute apple juice if needed. Makes the whole house smell wonderful and festive!

**MAKES
8 (4-OUNCE)
SERVINGS**

Apple cider, 1 gallon (substitute: apple juice)

2–6 cinnamon sticks

1 apple

1 orange or lemon

——

Equipment/Supplies

Medium pot (8 cups)

Chopping board

Chef's knife

Ladle (substitute: mug, handled cup)

Spoon holder or saucer for ladle

Tea cups, mugs, or disposable hot cups

1. Combine in a medium pot:
   Apple cider, 1 gallon (substitute: apple juice)
   2–6 cinnamon sticks
   Tip: If desired, add one cinnamon stick per person.

2. Slice into rings and use 2–3 of the most attractive slices (eat or save the rest for another use):
   1 apple
   1 orange or lemon

3. Simmer covered on Low, stirring occasionally, until steam rises.

4. If not serving immediately, cover and reheat just prior to serving.

5. To serve, ladle into cups or mugs. If desired, add a cinnamon stick, apple, and/or orange slice into each serving.

4 pm

As soon as the turkey comes out, add in another oven rack and heat up extra Sausage Stuffing, the Green Bean Casserole, and the Sweet Potato Soufflé. Remove the Cranberry Sauce, Bourbon Pecan Pie, and Pumpkin Pie and allow them to come to room temperature. Crank up the heat on the potatoes.

Lift the turkey onto a chopping board. Now you have the pan juices you need to make the Turkey Gravy.

TURKEY GRAVY

I have always been the official gravy maker and cream whipper in our household. My mom taught me how to make gravy from pan drippings and though it took a while to master, this skill has served me well on many occasions.

**MAKES
ABOUT 2 ½ CUPS**

½ cup flour mixed with water

Pan drippings

2 cups water

Equipment/Supplies

Mug or small bowl

Teaspoon

Liquid measuring cup, glass

Roasting pan or small pot (4 cups)

Gravy boat

Small ladle or spoon

1. In a mug or small bowl, mix together with a teaspoon to make a semi-liquid paste:
   ½ cup flour mixed with water
   Tip: You do not need to measure these amounts precisely.

2. Place the roasting pan on top of two burners and pour in:
   2 cups water
   Tip: If you prefer, pour pan drippings and water mixture into a small pot.

3. Turn heat to Medium Low and use a metal spatula to scrape the browned bits off the bottom. If using the roasting pan, you may need to use two burners.

4. Begin pouring in the flour mixture little by little, stirring with the spatula to dissolve lumps.

5. When all the flour mixture has been added, turn heat to Medium. Continue stirring until gravy reaches desired consistency, about 5 minutes. If gravy does not thicken properly, make and add more flour and water mixture.

6. Taste and if needed, add more seasoning. If too salty, make and add more flour and water mixture.
   Salt and pepper

7. Pour gravy into the glass measuring cup and transfer it to a gravy boat or small bowl placed on top of a saucer (to avoid drips) with a small ladle or spoon.

5:30 pm

After dinner, remove the chilled bowl and beaters to whip up (pun intended) this final recipe.

Pro tip: Using a wire whisk instead of an electric mixer is a great workout for the flexor and extensor muscles.

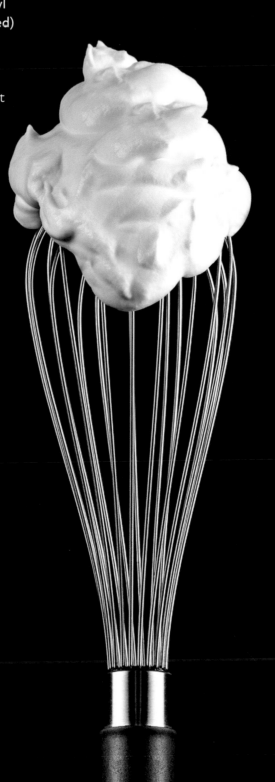

WHIPPED CREAM

For best results, chill a clean metal bowl and wire beaters or whisk at least one hour in advance by placing them in the refrigerator after the turkey goes in the oven. Powdered sugar is preferable, though white sugar will also work.

**MAKES
1 CUP**

1 cup heavy whipping cream

3 tablespoons powdered sugar (also labeled confectioners sugar)

___

Equipment/Supplies

Mixing bowl

Electric mixer or wire whisk

Liquid measuring cup, glass

Measuring spoons

Rubber spatula

Small serving bowl

Tablespoon

1. Take chilled bowl and wire beaters or whisk out of the refrigerator and place in the bowl:
1 cup heavy whipping cream

2. Using an electric mixer on Medium or a wire whisk, beat in a circular motion until soft peaks form.
   - With a mixer, this generally takes 5–6 minutes.
   - With a whisk, it should take about 10 minutes and you get the added benefit of building arm strength.
   Tip: If you beat the cream past stiff peaks and it begins turning into butter, add a few more tablespoons of cream and beat again.

3. When you lift the beaters out, the cream should be stiff enough to drop by dollops on to a piece of pie.

4. Fold in with a rubber spatula:
3 tablespoons powdered sugar (also labeled confectioners sugar)

5. Taste and add more sugar as needed until desired sweetness is reached.

6. Scrape into a small bowl (like a soup bowl) with the rubber spatula.

7. Pass whipped cream on the side with pie.

You did it!

If you made it to this page, and more importantly, you cooked one or all of these dishes, you've earned my praise and perhaps a nice nap as well. Very proud of you.

Happy Feasting!

CHECKLISTS

I use these checklists myself every year. You might want to
make copies or use a pencil. Check with the publisher to see if
downloads are available. See the Sunday chapter for pictures
of commonly used items. In this chapter, you will find:

Cooking Equipment/Baking Supplies
Take a look at what you have to determine if you have substitutes
for the needed items or if there are any tools you want to invest
in. Turkey baster, anyone?

Serving Essentials
Use this list to plan ahead for serving everything. There are
disposable versions of many items if you need them.

Shopping List
Check off what you already have, double ingredients as needed,
find substitutes, and take this list with you to get everything
you need.

COOKING EQUIPMENT

POTS & PANS
○ Small pot (4 cups)
○ Medium pot (8 cups)
○ Large pot (16+ cups)
○ 1–2 skillets (preferably cast iron)
○ Square pan (8-inch) or loaf pan
○ Baking dish (9 x 13 inch) or medium cast iron skillet
○ Roasting pan (12 x 17 inch) or rimmed baking sheet
○ Roasting rack (substitute: use roughly chopped onions or carrots instead)

KNIVES & CARVING
○ Bread knife (substitute: serrated steak knife)
○ Carving fork
○ Carving knife
○ Chef's knife
○ Chopping board
○ Paring knife

UTENSILS & SMALL APPLIANCES
○ Can opener
○ Colander (substitute: slotted spoon or tongs)
○ Cooking or meat thermometer
○ Electric mixer or wire whisk
○ Kitchen shears or scissors
○ Metal spatula
○ 1–2 mixing bowls, large
○ Potato masher
○ Timer (may use phone timer)
○ Vegetable peeler

TURKEY ESSENTIALS
○ 6 metal pins (substitute: kitchen twine)
○ Turkey baster (recommended investment)

BAKING SUPPLIES
○ Aluminum foil
○ Dry measuring cups (set of 4)
○ Liquid measuring cup, glass
○ Measuring spoons (set of 4)
○ Parchment paper
○ 2 pie pans (8-inch)
○ Pie weights, dried beans, or uncooked rice (2–4 cups)
○ 2 pizza or cookie sheets (preferably round)
○ Rolling pin (substitute: food safe rollers, straight-sided drinking glass)
○ Rubber spatula
○ Wooden spoon

OPTIONAL ITEMS
○ Box grater (if not buying shredded cheese)
○ Containers or resealable bags for food storage
○ Pastry brush
○ 2 wire cookie racks

Tip: Baking pans are typically metal, baking dishes are glass or ceramic. Disposable versions are widely available. If using a disposable roasting pan, use two pans nested inside each other to make it easier to lift and carry.

SERVING ESSENTIALS

PLACE SETTINGS
- ○ 4–12 Place settings, including:
  - • Dinner plates
  - • Silverware—dinner fork, butter knife, teaspoon
  - • Water glasses
- ○ 4–12 napkins (cloth if possible)
- ○ 4–12 dessert forks
- ○ 4–12 dessert plates
- ○ Salt and pepper grinders or shakers

SERVING DISHES
- ○ 5 trivets, or more (substitute: oven mitts, folded kitchen towels)
- ○ 1 large serving platter or tray
- ○ 2 large serving bowls
- ○ 2 small soup bowls
- ○ 1 gravy boat (substitute: small bowl, large mug)

SERVING UTENSILS
- ○ 1 large serving fork or pair of tongs
- ○ 4 large serving spoons
- ○ 2 tablespoons
- ○ 1 small ladle or tablespoon
- ○ 1–2 knives
- ○ 1–2 spatulas

BEVERAGES
Based on 2–3 (8-ounce) servings per person
- ○ 1 medium ladle (substitute: handled cup or mug)
- ○ 4–12 mugs or hot drink cups
- ○ 1–2 water pitchers (2 quarts/ 64 ounces each)
- ○ 1 package beverage napkins (small square napkins)

OPTIONAL ITEMS
- ○ Ice bucket or large bowl for ice
- ○ Ice tongs or large spoon
- ○ 4–12 extra glasses or disposable cups —to use before dinner
- ○ Tray for pitchers and glasses/cups
- ○ 4–12 wine glasses
- ○ Corkscrew or wine opener

SHOPPING LIST

Shop local and organic whenever possible.

BREAD / CANS / JARS
- ○ Bread, 2 loaves (1 white and 1 wheat, or both wheat)
- ○ Cream of Mushroom soup, 1 can (10.5-ounce)
- ○ French fried onions, 1 can (6-ounce)
- ○ Pumpkin, 1 can (15-ounce)

BAKING
- ○ Agave syrup, 1 cup
- ○ Brown sugar, light or dark, 4 cups (substitute: white sugar)
- ○ Bourbon, ¼ cup (optional)
- ○ Condensed milk, 1 can (14-ounce)
- ○ Flour, 6 cups (substitute: 2–4 premade pie crusts)
- ○ Maple syrup, ½ cup
- ○ Olive oil for sautéing
- ○ Pecans—chopped, 2 cups (8 ounces)
- ○ Pecans—halves, 1 cup (about 60 halves)
- ○ Powdered sugar, ¼ cup (also labeled confectioners sugar)
- ○ Vanilla, 1 ½ teaspoons
- ○ Walnuts, chopped, ½ cup (4 ounces)

SPICES / GARNISH
- ○ Cinnamon, 2 sticks or more
- ○ Pepper, ground
- ○ Pumpkin pie spice or 1–2 teaspoons of these ground spices:
  - • Allspice
  - • Cinnamon
  - • Cloves
  - • Ginger
  - • Nutmeg
- ○ Sage, dried
- ○ Sea salt
- ○ Thyme, dried

PRODUCE
- ○ Apple, 1 red or green (such as Fuji, Gala, or Granny Smith)
- ○ Celery, 2 bunches
- ○ Cranberries, 12 ounces (1–2 bags, depending on brand)
- ○ Garlic, 4 cloves
- ○ Green beans, 1 pound
- ○ Herbs, fresh (optional but recommended for cooking or decoration
  - • Rosemary
  - • Sage
  - • Thyme
- ○ Onions, 2 yellow
- ○ Orange, 1 navel
- ○ Potatoes, medium, 8 red or 4 russet
- ○ Sweet potatoes, 5 medium

TURKEY
SAVVY

DAIRY
- ○ Milk, ½ cup
- ○ Butter, 10 sticks (4-ounce sticks, 48 ounces total)
- ○ Cheddar cheese, shredded, ½ cup (4 ounces)
- ○ Sour cream, ½ cup (4 ounces)
- ○ Whipping cream, 1 cup (8 ounces)

MEAT / EGGS
- ○ Eggs, 1 dozen (you will have extras)
- ○ Pork sausage, 2 pounds (commonly found in the deli case, get two 16-ounce tubes, 32 ounces total)
- ○ Turkey, 14–16 pounds, frozen or fresh

BEVERAGES
(for 4 guests based on 2 servings per person, 8-ounces each)
- ○ Water, 2 quarts tap or bottled (64 ounces)
- ○ Apple cider, 1 gallon (substitute: apple juice)
- ○ Sparkling water, 2 or more bottles (64 ounces or 4 liters)
- ○ White wine, 2 or more bottles (such as Chardonnay, Rosé, or Sauvignon Blanc)

OPTIONAL ITEMS
- ○ Ice (typically comes in bags of 5 pounds or more)
- ○ Parsley, ground or fresh (for garnish)
- ○ Turkey baster (recommended investment)
- ○ Metal pins or cooking twine
- ○ Cooking/meat thermometer
- ○ Disposable pans—roasting, pie pans, loaf pan, square pan, etc.
- ○ Aluminum foil
- ○ Parchment paper
- ○ Wax paper
- ○ Paper towels
- ○ Containers or resealable bags for food storage
- ○ Kitchen gloves

OPTIONAL DECORATIONS
- ○ Candles, 2 or more tapers or votives
- ○ Decorative mini-pumpkins and/or gourds, assorted
- ○ Small vases, 1–2 vases (substitute: jam or mustard jars)

INDEX

CKNOWLEDGEMENTS

This project would not have been possible without the creative vision and extraordinary talent of Roseline Seng of Rose Line Design. I could not have asked for a more ideal collaborator, sounding board, and napkin ironer. You took a massive amount of information, organized it, and infused it with such panache. I am eternally grateful that you were up for the challenge. Can't wait for the next one!

We had the great fortune to partner with food photographers Sofia Felguérez and Alex Monfort at The Photo Pot; food stylist Nicole Kruzick at Belly Food Style; and printer Marx Ortega at Marina Graphic Center. Your considerable talents helped us fulfill our vision for this book.

This book was also written for Sam's cousins: Emily, David, Hannah, and Elizabeth Chun; Stacey Dubak and George Mackool; Jillian Stubbs and Jaclyn Sroda. Here's to many more years of feasting! To our families, who bravely supported this journey, in addition to eating a lot of turkey: Annie, Christopher, Jonathan, and Carrie Chun; Albert Williams, Cindy and Tom Hill, Becky Sroda, and Todd Williams—you are simply the best.

Mahalo nui loa to Liz Cavanaugh, Patty Chan, Deborah Chang, Liz Dawrs, Laurie Fagen, Diana Folsom, and Jane Kim—your encouragement and input meant the world to me. Heartfelt appreciation to my niece Lizzie for recipe testing; Nini Lieberman for the recipe and caring spirit; and Raymond Salas for the pro DJ hacks. Grateful to Kate Zentall, my UCLA X Creative Nonfiction cohort, and online writing group members who reviewed prior versions of this material. Special thanks to Kemal, Julian, and Ruby Rachman for sharing Roseline and supporting our project.

In memory of Alfred Y. H. Chun, Shirley M. Williams, Sheena H. C. Chun, and Marcelyn M. Kropp—you will ever be in my heart.

Glenn and Samuel Williams, forever the great loves of my life, you are the reason this book exists. While Sam was the catalyst, Glenn supplied hard-won expertise, real time coaching, and last-minute turkey wrangling. You inspire me every day.

May your plates overflow with all your favorite things!

Jessica C. Williams, author of *Turkey Savvy*, is a writer, course creator, and organizational effectiveness consultant who guides clients on transformational change journeys. Williams has extensive experience writing and editing custom corporate communications and training material. Her work has appeared in multiple local and nonprofit publications. Born and raised in Honolulu, Hawai'i, she graduated from the University of Hawai'i at Mānoa and the University of Southern California. Jessica lives in Venice Beach, California with her husband and son.

Roseline Seng, art director and designer of *Turkey Savvy*, is the founder of Rose Line Design, an award-winning graphic design studio specializing in branding, marketing, and book design. Born and raised in Singapore, she graduated from the Otis/Parsons School of Design in Los Angeles, California. She has taught at Otis and UCLA Extension, and her work has been recognized in several distinguished design publications.